NHL worldwide icehockey Dallas Stars indiany

Peter Oberfrank – Hunziker

Impressum:

Bibliografische Information der Deutschen
Nationalbibliothek: Die Deutsche
Nationalbibliothek verzeichnet diese Publikation in
der Deutschen Nationalbibliografie; detaillierte
bibliografische Daten sind im Internet über
www.dnb.de abrufbar.

© 2022 Peter Oberfrank – Hunziker
Herstellung und Verlag
BoD – Books on Demand, Norderstedt

ISBN 9783755791218

MIX
Papier aus verantwortungsvollen Quellen
Paper from responsible sources
FSC® C105338

indiany colourfull stary is for me Peter Oberfrank -
Hunziker wonderful drawing and being happy and
worldwide journeying and NHL Icehockeyplaying
ever and technical workying ever and remembering
and being with my NHL art naming unique indiany
being icehockeyplayer NHL Dallas Stars indiany
Peter Oberfrank - Hunziker

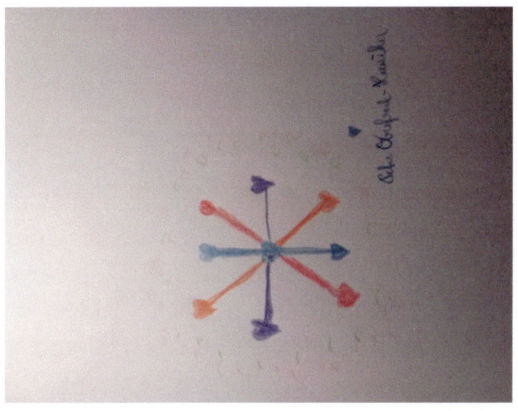

NHL Washingtoni is also being hearty with all my
NHL art naming Indiany icehockey
ⓒ
NHL all star indiany
Peter Oberfrank – Hunziker

NHL Icehockey all star Indiany me being with my original name Peter Oberfrank - Hunziker and my NHL art naming like 24 Perthaler and NHL 79 Ross Colton and ewigi indiany and tampy star and Joe Thornton and 99 Wayne Gretzky and Krutov and 20 Henrique Lundyvist and NHL happy joyy and NHLY happy indiany and newyorkranges and 93 Zibanejad and NHL all star and NHL Washingtoni and 8 Ovechkin and 77 Oshie and NHL 16 Kevin Lavallee and 47 Martin St. Louis and NHL 19 Steven Yzerman and wingerlen and Detroity and Devils and Team Canada and 87 Sydney Crosby and Modano and Lemieux and Heatley and 72 Filip Chytil and 28 Giroux and NHL St. Louis Blues indiany blue and Dury and 4 Neil Belland and all sports indiany and NHL Stanley cup champions winning ever with all NHL teams and captainying all NHL teams ever and kingsy and 9 Adrian Kempe and Pavelski and NHL great perthalerlen at Alpensee indiany and stary indiany and Pietrangelo and Backes and NHL Las Vegas Golden Knights star and Yagr and NHL icehockey Montreal Canadiens indiany and nhling and NHL shop and NHL museum and NHL festivals and NHL icehockeyparty and NHL Washington Capitol

indiany NHL Lemieux and NHL 86 Kucherov
and CSKA and indiany and Yevgeni Malkin
worldwide journeying and great partying und
einzigartig and unique and happy stary
indiany Peter Oberfrank - Hunziker

ॐ

ಁ

ౘ

☺

☺

�

ॐ

ॐ

ෆ

☺

ॐ

ॐ

ඟ

ॐ

ෆ

ॐ

ඕ

ॐ

ॐ

ෆ

ॐ

�

ౘ

ෞ

ॐ

ॐ

ॐ

ഈ

ඖ

ᢍ

�

�…

ॐ

ᴪ

ఞ

ॐ

ഈ

☺

�

ӫ

�| ఈ |

ඏ

ॐ

ගි

ఌ

ඣ

ॐ

ಠ

ఌ

ఉ

ကဲ

ॐ

ഔ

ॐ

�

ῶ

ඕ

ⓒ

ॐ

ෝ

ఊ

ॐ

ॐ

ॐ

ౠ

ஓ

ထ

ॐ

ഞ

ఈ

ౝ

ෆ

ॐ